REFLECTIONS & MEDITATIONS
ON THE
LOVE OF GOD

William J. Wardle

Pen Press Publishers Ltd
London

© William J. Wardle 2000

All rights reserved.

First published in Great Britain by
Pen Press Publishers Ltd
39-41 North Road
London
N7 9DP

ISBN 1 900796 37 6

A catalogue record for this book
is available from the British Library

Cover design by Catrina Sherlock
From an original idea by William J. Wardle

Dedicated to

Sancta Maria Abbey, Nunraw, Scotland.

Prologue

This collection of reflections and meditations is made up from jottings in my pocket book and are much the same as we all make in our hearts every time we turn to Our Lord in prayer.

I am sure that if you keep a spiritual journal you are able to look back at your entries and clearly recall moments of discovery. The jottings that come together to make this collection each represent a moment of awareness.

As I wrote the reflections to introduce the meditations, my mind continually recalled phrases from the Gospels and the Letters of St Paul. You will find them threaded throughout the reflections, and I hope they may act as familiar milestones leading you into the meditations that follow.

The meditations have been written 'on my way through life', which is for me a continual path of discovery regarding my faith and my life. You may not relate to them all but, at the outset, I would like to thank you for letting me share them with you, for by so doing I may yet come to acknowledge them as an expression of my own faith, and by making such an acknowledgement may yet awaken to the full reality of Christ's love in my life.

| Collection of Reflections and Meditations | Page No. |

On The Love of God — 5

The Mantle of Your Presence
Haunted by Nostalgia
Dispirited Unease
Night on The Island
The Generosity of Love
The Jealousy of Love's Possession
Heavenly Father
The Open Doors of The Tabernacle
The Companionship of Awakening
The Dream of The Desert

On The Longing for God — 19

In Heaven Here on Earth
Inner Vision of My Soul
The Road that Leads to Calvary
The Sacrifice so Long Resisted
The Riches of Your Poverty
Your Faithfulness
The Path to Heaven
A Moment of Eternity
The Solitude of God
The Ocean of Desire

On The Journey to God — 33

Naught to Trust
Voice of Pride
Wilderness of Emotion
Essence of Atonement
Servant of My Promise

Silence of Gethsemane
Water of Life
Steps of The Sanctuary
Sacrament of The Moment
Summit of Holiness

Of A Prisoner of Eternity 55

Prisoner of Eternity
Wondrous Divinity
Freedom of the Kingdom of Love
Companion in Time
The Man I Feared to Be
A Man Awakes
Kinship with Immortality
Heart's Desire
Image of The Man of Heaven
Eternal Regeneration

On The Unknown Reality 69

Living Faith
Compulsion of Love
Land of Lost Horizons
Need of God
Down by The Shore
Your Pain
A Particle of Love
Servant of Your Necessity
You Know It Lord
Unknown Reality

Seasonal Meditations 85

Queen of Heaven
Universal Mother of Salvation

The Star of Immortality
A Child of God
The Tapestry of God
A Bystander
Silhouette of God
In The Shadow of The Cross
In the Palm of My Hand
On the Road to Emmaus
The Seamless Robe of Grace
The Essence of Your Soul
Atlas of The World

Latest addition "Unknown Reality" July 1998

On The Love of God

Introduction

Opening Prayer

1. The Mantle of Your Presence

2. Haunted by Nostalgia

3. Dispirited Unease

4. Night on The Island

5. The Generosity of Love

6. The Jealousy of Love's Possession

7. Heavenly Father

8. The Open Doors of The Tabernacle

9. The Companionship of Awakening

10. The Dream of The Desert

Closing Prayer

Introduction

On the path through life, we often stop along the way to pick up pebbles, turning them over in our hands. Many of these pebbles find their way home in our coat pockets, and are kept as little reminders.

These meditations are like those pebbles, collected on life's path as little reminders of the Love of God.

Each meditation takes the form of a thought poem introduced by a brief reflection: a few moments of silence follow before the next reflection which picks up the thought and carries it into the next poem.

There are ten linked meditations forming a little rosary of beads of thought for turning over in our hands, like those pebbles.

The meditations begin and end with a prayer.

Lord Jesus,

may the reflections of Your love
shine upon our hearts,
and the wonder of Your being
entrance our minds,
that our spirits may be raised
into the joy of Your presence,
as we pray
through the inspiration of the Holy Spirit.

Amen.

The Mantle of Your Presence

During His life on earth, Jesus would withdraw from the crowds and the demands of His mission to mankind, and retire into the silence of the hills to be still in the presence of His Heavenly Father. As we unite in prayer let us withdraw from the external pressures of our lives and enter into this stillness and find our heart which lies deep within us, as we are enfolded in the mantle of His presence.

Luke 6:12 Jesus prays in solitude
T Merton: Contemplative Prayer.. "find our heart"

I love to feel the mantle of Your presence
As I close my mind to the tumult of my life,
And find my heart deep within my being
Where it lies hidden in obscurity.

As I let fall the fabrication of my life
A final shiver acknowledges my nakedness,
And numb heart awakens to its identity
In the reality of Your living presence.

In this awareness all I can do
Is own my nothingness, and wonder
That despite myself You enfold my being
In the mantle of Your presence.

Let me remain in the silence of Your tomb
Awaiting the dawning of the day
When You will roll away my heart of stone
And reveal the glory of Your presence.

Haunted by Nostalgia

During the day we are not able to retire into silence as often as we might wish, and there are times when we feel an aching nostalgia for prayer, a sense of need deep within our being. It may be that we feel a pressing desire to set our tasks aside and walk with Peter across the waters of life in answer to Christ's call; or it may be that we quietly sigh in the midst of our duties, in our desire to be held and blessed as a child in Christ's arms. In our own individual way, we feel the pressure of this desire as we go about our daily lives, haunted by nostalgia for prayer.

Math 14:22 Jesus calls Peter from across the water
Mark 10:13 Jesus blesses little children

I love to feel the pressure of each passing moment
As You haunt my spirit with nostalgia for prayer,
With the urgent need for the embrace of Your Presence,
Pressing me to withdraw to the sanctuary of my soul.

I long to respond to the echo of Your Voice
Calling to me from the far shore of the lake,
Bidding me leave the tending of my nets
To step out upon the eternal waters of life.

To reach out and touch the power of Your Hand,
The Hand that feeds me with mysteries of life,
To stand as a man before You, remembering a child
Your Hand laid upon him with Your promise of heaven.

Quietly I return to my nets by the lakeside,
Bending my will to the tasks there before me,
My heart suspended in silent adoration,
Haunted by nostalgia for the echo of Your Voice.

Dispirited Unease

Each and every day of our life, there are moments when that sense of nostalgia gives way to unease: we lose that sense of spiritual consolation and feel the weight of anxiety and apprehension, for there is always a corner of the lake where the windstorms blow. But it is our joy then to recall that Christ is with us, for even though He may appear to be asleep, He is rebuking the wind and the waves, calming the storms that arise through our restless wills. Let us pray that our faith may be strengthened and our wills redirected towards Him when we suffer dispirited unease.

Luke 12:22 Jesus tells His disciples not to worry
Mark 4:35 Jesus stills a storm

I love to recall to my spirit the depth of Your love
As dispirited unease troubles the surface of my soul,
And rise above the struggle of my restless will,
Returning to Your care the providence of my life.

I pause to lift my head above the windswept sea
And redirect my way to the haven of my desire,
This voyage through life to lead to Your purposed end,
Else all I will have lived for is a life in vain.

Against this soul distress and spirit of unease
I abandon my restless will in the stillness of faith,
Releasing my anxious spirit on the wings of prayer
As You breath into my being the life of Your Spirit.

And then I recover that secret enhancement of soul,
That awareness of Your Presence each moment of life;
My soul You rescue from its fear and apprehension,
Freeing my spirit from the shades of unease.

Night on The Island

Just as there are times when our spirit is uneasy through our inner restlessness, there are times when our soul is burdened by the many pressures and demands of our life that seem too great, and we feel anguish and distress. It is only when we retreat to our island of solitude that we are able to see that our anguish is occasioned by conflicts that are within us. It is then that our mood changes as we come face to face with our spiritual despondency, and come to the realisation and the acknowledgement that we are indeed poor stewards of the talents that our Saviour has given us; and then in the silence, we wait in tearful longing for Christ's coming to us in the night on the island.

Math 25:14 Parable of the talents

I love that moment when I hear Your footsteps
Crossing over the bridge on to my island of solitude,
Treading the palm branches I have strewn on the way,
A greeting prepared for Your visit long awaited.

You will find me tearful with much apprehension,
The burden You gave me weighing heavily upon me.
The talents You provided cast too far and wide,
Neither merit nor gain have I obtained for You.

All that You have given me in trust to endeavour
Is despoiled in the hands I hold out before You.
Despairing at my stewardship I weep on my island
Waiting for Your visit and the words that You bring.

You command me to love You and trust in Your Name;
You bid me remember the night of Your anguish,
Your tears in the darkness that brought light to the world:
So my spirit reawakens as night passes on the island.

The Generosity of Love

It is no easy matter to rise above despondency of spirit when Christ's demands on our life seem so great: it takes spiritual courage to watch for Christ during the night on the island. And even when the night passes, we shall often wonder if we will ever come to fully respond to the demands of Christ's love. It was in anticipation of Christ's call to be a disciple that Peter cried out in anguish, "Go away from me, Lord, for I am a sinful man". Such was his sense of unworthiness and inner dread at what Christ's call would mean for him. And yet, when his will hesitated and his faith weakened, Peter was soon to discover the wonderful generosity of Our Saviour's love, as Christ gently drew from him his confession, "Lord, you know everything; you know that I love You". As we struggle to maintain our spiritual courage let us remember the generosity of love.

Luke 5:4 Jesus calls Peter
John 21:15 Peter's confession

I love to wonder at the generosity of Your Love
As I struggle to maintain the surety of my faith:
Knowing that Your Hand is outstretched to guide me
Despite the hesitation and the frailty of my will.

I venture forth in Your Name at the dawn of each day,
Knowing that I am consecrating my life to You;
But my soul suffers anguish at the pressure of Your Hand
As You command the use of the gifts You have given me.

Have mercy Lord, my strength is but clay in Your Hand,
Your heavenly power too great for my poor soul to bear:
For Your great love demands the generosity of my will,
The very gift of all that I am and might yet become.

Even when I respond to the challenge of Your Will
I am living by the blind inspiration of my heart;
Yet as often as I fear that my faith is but vain
You renew my frail heart in the generosity of love.

The Jealousy of Love's Possession

It is when our hearts are filled with the generosity of Christ's love that we cry out with Peter, "Lord, you know everything; you know that I love You", and our hearts are given to Him and are no longer our own: we become the possession of God's love. Such love is all powerful, freeing us from our own wills and the emotions of self, but it is also a jealous love demanding our constancy. We are overwhelmed at such intensity of love and at the realisation that our consecration means so much to God. Let our hearts tremble with joy in the face of the jealousy of love's possession.

John 21:15 Peter's confession
John 21:20 Jesus and the beloved disciple

I love to feel the power of Your Almighty Hand
As Your jealous love takes possession of my heart,
Freeing and guarding me from the emotions of self,
Drawing me yet deeper into Your heavenly embrace.

I bow down before You in humble submission,
Overwhelmed at such intensity of love;
Fearful at the power of such possession
In my small perspective of the meaning of love.

Such is Your response to my tremulous will,
Informing my heart of the depth of Your love;
Trembling with joy I realize with awe
That my consecration is the desire of your heart.

Knowing and trusting Your impression on my soul,
I reach out to embrace the reality of Your love,
Confessing my hesitancy and years of self-doubt,
Treasuring Your jealousy of possession of my heart.

Heavenly Father

In what words can we respond to so powerful, so jealous and so loving a God? How may we approach Him? This is the question that the disciples asked, as they struggled for a way to approach 'The Mighty God': "Lord, teach us to pray". Jesus opened our way to God with the most treasured of all words, "Father", making us thereby children of God. There is no greater need for us than to be able to respond and to pray to God, and it is the greatest release and joy for the soul to pray in the way Our Saviour taught us to pray to the Heavenly Father.

Math 6:5 Jesus teaches His disciples how to pray

I love to worship You Father
And raise my soul to Heaven,
I pray to You for holiness
As I long for Christ my Saviour.

Grant me the grace to consecrate
My loving heart and will to You,
One with the angels and saints in Heaven
Praising the glory of Your Name.

Feed me this day with the Bread of Life,
The most precious gift of Christ Your Son;
Purify me by this heavenly food,
Grant me Your healing and forgiveness.

So fill me with love as I turn to You,
That I may bless all those who harm me;
And say that I may not be overwhelmed
But stand before You in innocence.

The Open Doors of The Tabernacle

As we pray in the way that Jesus taught us, and as we live out our lives in His Presence, we become increasingly aware that we owe everything to Jesus. He is the fulfilment of His Heavenly Father's love. Our happiness is the fulfilment of our life through our faith in Him: our hope is the fulfilment of our faith in everlasting life with Him. He is the love of the Father and in His life's sacrifice, He has given to us the greatest of all testaments of that love in the new and everlasting covenant of His Body and Blood. There can be no greater joy for us than to kneel before the Blessed Sacrament and adore Him, and to carry our living expectation out into the world from the open doors of the tabernacle.

John 16:27 Jesus confirms His disciples' belief
John 6:35,51 Jesus, the Bread of Life

I love to gaze upon the open doors
As the priest brings forth the Bread of Life,
And join the line of faithful pilgrims
Receiving Christ our Risen Lord.

As I draw near it is as if
Christ's Resurrection is portrayed,
For the open doors reveal the tomb
With the linen cloths surrounding.

And later in the darkened church
I kneel before the doors now sealed,
In silent adoration, waiting
In the garden at Christ's Sepulchre.

Then returning to the daily toil
I carry that great expectation,
For in lowly garb within our world
The Risen Christ is there to greet us.

The Companionship of Awakening

It was in the early hours of the morning that our Risen Saviour greeted Mary Magdalene, His Resurrection heralding a new dawn for each one of us. Each new day is a renewal of that greeting, and how great is our joy as we awaken from sleep to the returning awareness of the reality of Christ's love. At that moment we rededicate ourselves anew, our hearts filled with reassurance, knowing that as the world awakens we will never be lost in life's crowded streets, but will be held in the intimacy of the companionship of awakening.

John 20:11 Jesus greets Mary Magdalene
Math 16:13 Peter's declaration

I love to feel that returning sense of Your Presence
As awareness of being floods in upon my waking mind,
And the reality of Your love entrances my soul
Filling my consciousness with living consolation.

Old fears and anxieties emerge confusedly from sleep,
Pressing shadows upon the softened tissues of my soul,
As out into the blessed stillness my spirit emerges
Renewing the loving prayer of my soul's dedication.

Such reassurance unfolds in my heart as it awakens
To the embrace of Your Spirit in the wonder of silence;
With prayers of dawn welcoming the light of Your love
I unite with Creation in its longing for redemption.

As the world then awakens I renew my consecration,
Person to Person in the sanctuary of Your Presence;
Never to be lost in the crowds or the noise of the day
But held in the intimacy of the companionship of awakening.

The Dream of The Desert

After the intimacy of Christ's companionship in our waking moments, we all have a sense of homelessness as we return to the duties of our life. He is with us and the reflections of His love are all around us, but nothing can compare with the loving consolation of intimate prayer. But He calls us to tend our nets and venture forth in His Name, to fulfil our life through our faith in Him. And so we journey on in our earthly pilgrimage across the desert of this life, but every now and then, in the face of our homelessness, we stop to gaze out across the abyss, shielding our eyes from the glare of the sun, and we dream, the dream of the desert.

John 14:1 "My Father's House"
T Merton: Contemplative Prayer.. "dread"

I love to dream from within the silence of my being
Of a world beyond the horizon of my knowing,
There the God of our life, from realms unseen,
Draws mankind to his eternal destiny.

Of a world beyond the desert of this life
With its high walled castles of insecurity,
Where man seeks to hide from the risk and dread
Of submission to the unknown mysteries of God.

That desert in which mankind must lose itself,
Where there are no footsteps in the sand
In which to place our tread, as we are drawn
By the Spirit into the interior of silence.

Only as we face our dread and risk our fate
Outside the walls of our fortified cities,
Will we discover the suffering breath of God,
God's love for man, the substance of our dream.

Lord Jesus,

may the reflections of Your love
shine upon our hearts,
and the wonder of Your being
entrance our minds,
that our spirits may ever dwell
in the joy of Your presence,
as we live
by the guidance of the Holy Spirit.

Amen.

On The Longing for God

Introduction

Opening Prayer

1. In Heaven Here on Earth

2. Inner Vision of My Soul

3. The Road that Leads to Calvary

4. The Sacrifice so Long Resisted

5. The Riches of Your Poverty

6. Your Faithfulness

7. The Path to Heaven

8. A Moment of Eternity

9. The Solitude of God

10. The Ocean of Desire

Closing Prayer

Introduction

We all have hidden treasure in our hearts, secret dreams and deep emotions, that brings us both joy and sadness, creating that strange inner tension that produces tears at a wedding: hidden treasure that colours the way we look at things and which reflects our own attitudes and desires; hidden and, most often, secret.

We are, perhaps, like a child that opens its secret casket of treasure when it is sure to be alone and chooses from amongst the hidden treasure a cherished thread of glass crystals, lifting them up to the light in order to catch the reflections. Holding them as they sparkle and watching as the colours change, secret images are awoken in the mind of the child.

These ten meditations are like those glass crystals, a thread of reflective images on the love and the longing for God, for holding up to the light to catch the reflections.

The meditations begin and end with a prayer.

Lord Jesus

may the light of Your Presence
shine within the sanctuary of our souls
filling our inner vision
with the radiance of Your Being,
that with unveiled faces
we may see the reflection of Your Glory
and be transformed into Your Image
through the working
of the Holy Spirit.

Amen.

In Heaven Here on Earth

As the days and the years of our life unfold, our confidence in the mercy and love of God becomes the most cherished of all our secret treasure. Whenever we retire into the silent confines of our heart, sighing for the intimacy of Our Saviour's loving presence, we experience true release for our soul as we lay our cares before Him and place our trust in His mercy and love, resting our weary head upon His shoulder and opening our heart to Him with confidence. In the stillness, our soul fills with Christ's love and with the longing that one day we may ever dwell with Him, for in His embrace our spirit is in Heaven here on earth.

John 14:6 I am the way, and the truth, and the life.
No one comes to the Father except through Me.

I love to attend upon You my Lord
Within the silent confines of my heart,
And feel Your heavenly love caressing
The careworn centre of my earthbound soul.

I rest my weary head upon Your shoulder
As You gently draw me to Your Heart of Love,
The secret embrace of Your living presence
Comforting my soul as I journey on.

You raise my eyes to Your heavenly altar
To gaze upon Your eternal sacrifice,
Nourishing my soul with Your Risen Life
Sustaining my faith on this path You trod.

You fill my soul with longing for Heaven
As the days and the years of my life unfold,
My heart overflows with love's tears of joy,
My spirit is in Heaven here on earth.

Inner Vision of My Soul

It is from within the sanctuary of our soul where our spirit dwells in Christ's Presence that life and light emanate and enlighten the consciousness of our being. If there is darkness within, there is no vision, no light to shine upon our life. Our Saviour brought the light from Heaven to fill our soul with the vision of His Glory and to reflect that light into the world of men. The more we become aware of the radiance of Christ's love deep within us, the greater our longing becomes that one day the revelation of the Godhead may fill the inner vision of our soul.

John 8:12 I am the light of the world. Whoever follows Me will never walk in darkness but will have the light of life.

I love the inner vision of my soul
Enrapt in wonder at Your Being,
Enlightened by Your heavenly light
Irradiating upon my perception.

Rising towards the etherial vision
Opalescent rays glaze my sight,
Reflecting their milky iridescence
Within the sanctuary of my soul.

My only consciousness of being
Is this light within the sanctuary,
Revealing there Your hidden presence
Enshrined upon the altar of my heart.

Beyond this earthly tabernacle
Where You dwell in mystic concealment,
May the revelation of Your Godhead
Fill the inner vision of my soul.

The Road that Leads To Calvary

As the inner vision of our soul fills us with longing for the revelation of the Godhead, the light it brings opens our eyes to the challenge of our vocation. We find ourselves standing alone upon the summit of our soul, as on a high mountain overlooking the world in which we live, without boundaries of time and space, able to view our earthly life from above the daily concerns that beset us. These moments of clear perception intoxicate and yet bewilder us, for they most often reveal to us our spiritual frailty and our hesitation to maintain our steps upon the road that leads to Calvary.

John 14:27 Peace I leave with you; My peace I give to you.
I do not give to you as the world gives. Do not let
your hearts be troubled, and do not let them be afraid.

I love to rise upon the summit of my soul
And drink from Your Chalice the intoxicating dew
That from the eternal dawn Your Breath distilled
For the life of the world upon the road to Calvary.

I look out upon the high mountain passes
And down to the valley beds below the screes,
I see the dangers that beset Your disciple
As he follows upon the road that leads to Calvary.

I am bewildered by the height and depth
And long to rise upon the drifting air,
To turn and leave untrod those fearsome paths
That brought Your life to death upon the road to Calvary.

I shiver at the chilling mountain air
And fearfully tremble at the sheer descent,
For I know my way is cast upon that scene
Where death gives life upon the road that leads to Calvary.

The Sacrifice so Long Resisted

Our road to Calvary reveals to us our frailty and we become acutely aware of the self-deception in our heart. We are afraid to make the complete gift of ourselves that Our Saviour desires, and we try to love and serve Him in our own way. As unworthy servants we find ourselves often on our knees before Our Almighty Master with our face in our hands, broken and exhausted as our every attempt to offer ourselves to Him fails to satisfy His desire for our love and leaves us burning with longing. The more we try to come close to the Lord the greater our anxiety becomes, closing us round in pain and darkness. We can only kneel before Him with all the burnt out embers of our soul, and with deep humility make our offering to Him of the sacrifice of our love, the sacrifice we have so long resisted.

John 12:25 Those who love their life lose it, and those who hate their life in this world will keep it for eternal life.

I love You more than my heart can bear,
The pain of loving hurts my conscious mind
And burdens my soul with restless longing
As I resist the sacrifice Your love desires.

I am too blinded by my vision of Your Glory
To see Your gentle guiding Light upon the way,
I strain my eyes to penetrate the darkness
But the window of my soul reflects my image.

I can withstand Your Mighty Love no longer
Exhausted as I am with ceaseless yearning,
I long to extinguish the fires of self-love
And offer to You the embers of my soul.

I kneel before You holding in my hands
A little casket of my whitened ashes
Burnt out by the flames of my desire,
The sacrifice of love so long resisted.

The Riches of Your Poverty

The sacrifice of love that we so long resisted releases our soul from our self-deceptions, but as we raise ourselves from the ashes we still encounter all the emotional needs and attachments that entangle our will, forming obstacles in our longing to attain true spiritual freedom to love God. Whilst we cling to our own sense of security, we fill our mind with distractions that prevent us from embracing the spirit of selflessness and inner poverty through which Christ's love flows. We hide behind the excuse of a loveless world in which Our Lord faced rejection, but we will only find release for our soul when we embrace His rejection and sufferings which alone open to us the treasure of the riches of His poverty.

John 12:26 Whoever serves Me must follow Me, and where I am, there will My servant be also. Whoever serves Me, the Father will honour.

I love to reach for the embrace of Your poverty,
Not permitting myself to deny Your pain
Nor concealing from my heart Your anguish
As You bore the rejection of mankind.

Deny me myself and my justifications
Releasing my soul from worldly distractions,
That my heart may escape from false consolation
To embrace man's burden of guilt and shame.

Free my heart from suffocating apathy
In which Your love is stifled as a yawn,
Open my soul to Your pain and Your suffering
That I may be enfolded in Your wounded heart.

Clothe my being in the white robes of salvation
That nakedness of soul may shame me no longer,
Grant me to desire but Your garland of thorns
That I may inherit the riches of Your poverty.

Your Faithfulness

As we embrace Christ's rejection and poverty of spirit we experience the deep vulnerability of Our Saviour. Each day we face the conflict He endured as spiritual values come up against the challenge of the values that dominate the world, a conflict which reproduces in our soul the life of Christ as His ministry carried Him through conflict and betrayal to His Death. Unlike Our Saviour we are too often afraid to be ourselves, afraid that the challenge will be too great for us to bear. We will only find the strength to be steadfast witnesses by imitating Our Lord, keeping before our eyes the Triumph of the Cross, never doubting the efficacy of our faith through which He will support us, provided we remain true to Him in selfless response to His faithfulness.

*John 15:19   Because you do not belong to the world,
              but I have chosen you out of the world -
              therefore the world hates you.*

I love to feel Your Hand constraining me
To rise up under the weight of the cross,
Causing me to share Your love's rejection,
Establishing my soul in faithfulness.

I long to give of my all yet fear to be
The loving soul You greet at dawn each day
With warm embrace of love by which I know
Your blessing on my way of innocence.

Conceal my diffidence and cover my pride
With the veil of the grace of humility,
For the secret strength of Your servant's love
Lies hidden within Your silent abjection.

May the love of Your Cross impress on my soul
A selfless response to love's sacrifice,
That I may bear the stigma of faith
As a steadfast witness to Your faithfulness.

The Path to Heaven

It is Christ's faithfulness that sustains us through the many challenges and conflicts that arise as we seek to follow and imitate Him in our life. The more firmly we place our feet on the path He trod, dedicating our life to Him, the closer we are drawn to Our Saviour, our own experience of His faithfulness raising our confidence and our hope in His promises, filling our heart with longing for eternal life. On this journey of faith we seek to free our spirit of encumbrances, to hold our few possessions lightly and our true affections deeply, in readiness for the day and the hour when we will take our final step, carrying with us only the treasure that is in our heart, upon the path to heaven.

> *John 14: 3* *And if I go and prepare a place for you,*
> *I will come again and will take you to Myself,*
> *so that where I am, there you may be also.*

I love to keep before my eyes
The hope of Heaven's blessing,
The fulfilment of this earthly life
Your promise of an eternal home.

To touch the transient things of earth
With hands that do not seek to retain,
That I might freely grasp the moment
With neither hesitation nor regret.

With heart cut loose from self desire
In freedom to love with true affection,
That I might carry into heaven
The treasury of a life's devotion.

To see these passing days as steps
Upon the vast eternal journey,
That my one desire may overreach the hour
Along the timeless path to Heaven.

A Moment of Eternity

It is only in moments of deep reflection that we sense the vastness of our eternal journey and the timelessness that extends beyond the confines of our life here on earth. There is one such moment, of the most unique significance, in which the whole meaning of life itself is focused. Raising our heart to God with longing to be enfolded in His eternal love, we come before the Risen Christ to worship and adore Him in the Blessed Sacrament and to receive Him in the most holy Eucharist; to hold in our hands for a moment in time the eternal treasure of God's love for us, the Body of Our Lord and Saviour. As we open the palms of our hands to receive the Host at the hands of His priest, there opens to us a moment of eternity.

John 6:51 I am the living bread that came down from heaven.
Whoever eats of this bread will live forever; and the
bread that I will give for the life of the world is My flesh.

I love to open the palms of my hands
In longing expectation of that moment
When before my eyes You come to me
Veiled in the mystery of the Eucharist.

I gaze in awe upon the Heavenly Host
In which by faith You reveal Your Presence
Bidding me take and eat this sacred food,
For This Is Your Body sacrificed for me.

I touch the Host with trembling fingers
And raise it to my expectant lips,
That I may receive the Bread of God
The food that endures for eternal life.

I fold in prayer these hands that held You
And raise my earthbound soul to Heaven,
My spirit filled with longing for salvation
Lost in wonder in a moment of eternity.

The Solitude of God

Secret moments of eternity take us beyond the customary path of life where we tread in the conscious certainty of our material universe, leading us to contemplate the mysteries of faith and life. It is in the silence and the darkness of the night that our being is enclosed in life's deepest mystery, the solitude (the deep and hidden presence) of God, into Whose Holy Presence we enter through the solitude of our own soul, that most essential aspect of our being which shadows us throughout our life and with which we come face to face at our death; the universal solitude of mankind before the Eternal Presence of God. Drifting into the unconsciousness of sleep with our heart centred on God, we touch upon the moment when we will pass for ever from this life, through our unconsciousness into the mysterious world of the Spirit, the eternal realms of our Risen Saviour, where our soul will be embraced within Christ's universal love of mankind in the eternal solitude of God.

*John 15: 9 As the Father has loved Me, so I have loved you;
    abide in My love.*

I love the still dark hours of the night,
Hidden from earthly light and passing shadows,
My soul drifting into eternal solitude
Deep in the shade of the Almighty.

As I fall through the silence to my rest,
My spirit stirs in unconscious depths
Rising to the embrace of heavenly repose
In the Sacred Heart of the Love of God.

Silently passing the watches of the night,
My soul touches the timelessness of eternity,
My spirit suspended in its guardian world
As my ageing body journeys on.

Life forces meet as daybreak returns
Reawakening the focused intent of life,
Recalling my spirit from the unknown realms
Of the eternal mystery of the solitude of God.

The Ocean of Desire

As we long for the fulfilment of heavenly love, dreaming of the land of far horizons on this vast eternal journey, we continually raise our soul to Christ Our Saviour. It is a voyage of life that carries us ever closer towards the day of our death, but the deeper our love grows, the greater our confidence becomes. Our Lord holds the compass on this journey and we are safe within His Hand if only we will abandon our life to Him and cast ourselves adrift upon the ocean of desire.

John 11:25 I am the resurrection and the life. Those who believe in Me, even though they die, will live, and everyone who lives and believes in Me will never die.

I love to cast myself adrift upon the ocean of desire
Abandoning my life to You upon the unfathomed sea of faith
And feel the surging currents of Your heavenly love
Drawing me ever onward to the land of far horizons.

May Your lights on my journey chart my path in the skies
Guiding my uncertainty through the darkest of nights,
May the breezes on the waters give life and true motion
To the urgency of faith and the longing of my love.

Steer an even course through the tempests of my life
That no unchartered regions may endanger hope or trust,
Beyond sight of land may your angels guard my progress
Watching and protecting this poor vessel of my love.

As the swell of the ocean lifts the bow of my prayers
May the breath of Your Spirit fill the sails of my heart
That my soul may surely find its true loving destination
The harbour of my dreams on this ocean of desire.

Lord Jesus

may the light of Your Presence
shine within the sanctuary of our souls
filling our inner vision
with the radiance of Your Being,
that with unveiled faces
we may reflect the brightness of Your Glory
and be transformed into Your Likeness
through the working
of the Holy Spirit.

Amen.

On The Journey to God

Introduction

Opening Prayer

1. Naught to Trust

2. Voice of Pride

3. Wilderness of Emotion

4. Essence of Atonement

5. Servant of My Promise

6. Silence of Gethsemane

7. Water of Life

8. Steps of The Sanctuary

9. Sacrament of The Moment

10. Summit of Holiness

Closing Prayer

Introduction

Our journey of faith, our quest for holiness, depends entirely upon a personal relationship, our relationship with God, deep in the centre of our being. There is in each one of us an awareness of this 'centre of solitude' within which we struggle with our humanity as we encounter Our Lord. St Paul reminds us that *once we were slaves to the elemental spirits of the world until God sent His Son to redeem us*. In Jesus rests all our confidence, our hope and our trust as we make this journey of faith.

These reflections and meditations, hesitating steps on the journey to God, invite us to consider our own inner path. This path can lead us through places of pain and loneliness, into chambers filled with the echoes of our life, but *as the Spirit of life in Christ Jesus sets us free* from our own self-possession, we are led into the centre of solitude wherein we encounter the Lord. Our loving Father *sent His Son in order to redeem us so that we might receive adoption as children:* and so, to make this journey we do not have to become a child of our imagination but simply a child of God.

There are ten reflections each introducing a short meditation, a decade from life's rosary, following this thread of thought through the hidden world of spiritual awareness into the centre of solitude within our soul, ten steps of discovery on the journey that leads us ever deeper into the love of God.

The journey begins and ends with a prayer.

Gal 4:3-5   Rom 8:2   Gal 4:5

Lord Jesus,

may the sound of Your Voice
break through the silence of our solitude,
and may the light of Your Presence
shine through the darkness of our vision,
that we may hear the promptings of grace
and walk in the knowledge of Your will
on this journey of faith
under the guidance of
the Holy Spirit.

Amen.

Naught to Trust

The first hesitating step *as a child of God is to be led by this spirit of adoption* to quieten all the self-doubt that echoes around our solitude, and to acknowledge to ourselves that we can make no progress on this journey until we have the courage to become the person we were made to be. What we are today is far from the image in which we were created. To be true to ourselves and to our Saviour *we must be renewed in the spirit of our minds and clothe ourselves with the new self, created according to the likeness of God in true righteousness and holiness.* We must work to restore the self-respect which we have lost, the cause of so much of our shame, *holding firm the confidence and the pride that belong to hope.* This can only be done by placing ourselves in the presence of Christ day by day, trusting in His deep love for us. As we unmask ourselves before Him, we confront our helplessness and our frailty, and our acts of presumption, and we realise that there is but naught to trust in us.

Rom 8:14-15   Eph 4:23-24   Heb 3:6

I love to believe that I can be myself
And not worry that I need a full rehearsal,
Not regretting that every word and action
Wasn't first considered and duly weighed.

It is nice to think that endless apologies
Are not to be written-in to all that I say,
That I can be truly the man that You made me
And please You dear Lord by just being Me.

If I place all I am before you each day,
And pray that I may live but simply for You,
Then maybe I will not so fear my shadow
Nor constantly wish to retrace my steps.

But what act of living excludes presumption?
And how may I trust myself to be?
Only in Your love dear Lord can I trust,
For there is but naught to trust in me.

Voice of Pride

As we acknowledge our frailty, we reason within ourselves as to the extent to which we are meant to act boldly and ask our Lord to keep us from acting presumptuously, *for if we who are nothing think we are something we deceive ourselves.* In the activity of each day there is little opportunity to stop and examine ourselves as to how we behave; we can only pray that the Lord will guide us by the path of His Will and grant us the grace we need to act according to His counsels. However, so often we forget our better intentions and whilst we *can will what is right, we cannot do it*, and we find ourselves responding to situations in ways which we would condemn in others. The chief cause is our pride, and it is self-pride that forms our first line of defence as we seek to justify our actions and avoid the embarrassment of humiliation or contradiction. *In our weakness we should not be proud, but we should only be proud of the things that show our weakness*, bowing before Our Lord in our abjection. Our self-respect can only be restored by such a response, else our embarrassment will continue to burn within us as we return to our solitude. Of all the voices that echo around the silence of solitude there is none more distressing to be heard than the anguished voice of pride.

Gal 6:3   Rom 7:18   2 Cor 11:30

I love to waken in the stillness of solitude
Deep in the forest where my spirit has roamed
And watch through the dawn as the vaporous air rises
Up through the trees to the rays of the sun.

In the dark night I heard the voice of anguish
Amid whispering curses avenging self-pride,
I saw tortured features tormented by scorn
Faces disfigured and twisted by bitterness.

I had stumbled on a path through the darkness of my soul
As I hearkened to the voices that echoed my dissent,
But the moment they spied me and rose from their prey
I fled from their evil, hiding deep in the forest.

It is thus that You find me in nakedness of shame
Trembling at the faces that mirrored my soul,
Seeking the humility to acknowledge my abjection,
To silence the echo of the anguished voice of pride.

Wilderness of Emotion

In our anguish we wait for the healing love of God, aware that we fail in our endeavours so easily when our emotions and self-pride get the better of us. Sometimes it seems that Our Lord allows us to enter into the darkness of despair at the edge of faith to cause us to leave behind the commotion of our senses and be still in order *to examine ourselves to see whether we are living in the faith*. In the depth of our despair, all justification falls away and we sense that He brought us to this place to begin again, to *work out our own salvation with fear and trembling, knowing that it is God who is at work in us enabling us to will and work for His good pleasure*. In this growing awareness of our faith we have the courage to rise up once more to the challenges that await us, for we realise that *whenever we acknowledge our weakness, then we are strong,* and are able to set out again on our journey, leaving all uncertainty behind us in the wilderness of emotion.

2 Cor 13:5   Phil 2:12-13   2 Cor 12:10

I love to find You in the wilderness of emotion
Where faith fills the void in the chasm of despair
But where hope with its dreams lies broken and scattered
Amidst the ruins of the temple in the wasteland of my soul.

It was Your loving Spirit that brought me to this wilderness
To wrestle with the beasts that are the heart's emotions,
To look down upon the empire of the vanity of Egypt,
And tread the great precipice at the very edge of faith.

You take me by the arm and draw me from the threshold,
Your embrace of love through the frailty of my being
Bringing all the comfort of longed-for reassurance
That only my Saviour God can ever give to me.

You guide me by the Spirit from this land of my exile
And lead me to the parting of the sea of my despair,
Before me lies uncharted the journey of my exodus
As the waters close behind me in the wilderness of emotion.

Essence of Atonement

The wilderness of emotion does not lead into the promised land: the route from Egypt takes us across the desert, for it is only as we desire to reach an understanding of the Divine Law that we begin our exodus from Egypt. We may have fled from our captors but we have yet to prove our fidelity, *to cleanse ourselves from every defilement of body and of spirit, making holiness perfect in the fear of God.* We need to find space in which to expand our will to love God, to confirm our intention and resolve, and to rediscover for ourselves the love of Christ. *He became like us so that He might be a merciful and faithful high priest in the service of God, to make a sacrifice of atonement for our sins.* In His act of atonement, Jesus gave His life for our salvation, and yet we have lived careless of His saving love. As if blown across by the sands of neglect and indifference in the desert of our life, we must now find and uncover the tomb of Our Lord's unrequited love that He may rise from the depths of our soul and dwell within us that we may become *the temple of the living God.* It is in His love alone that we will find the essence of atonement.

2 Cor 7:1   Heb 2:17   2 Cor 6:16

I love to enter the desert of my exodus
Where earthly comfort dies a barren death,
And where my soulful sighs in deepest longing
Find the silent ways of healing solitude.

Desire turns inward consuming with fire
The appetite that hungers for mortal consolation,
And vision is darkened to my earthly gaze
As the mirage of the world fades away.

The darkness conceals my path through the desert
Which I must follow in the blindness of faith,
Until I have bruised the soles of my feet
On the hidden tomb of Our Lord's unrequited love.

And then I shall behold My Saviour rising in glory,
No longer buried in time or shrouded in eternity
But rising from the depths of the temple of my soul,
For there I shall have found Him, the Essence of Atonement.

Servant of My Promise

Our journey through the desert is over, for we have there discovered for ourselves the love of Our Saviour deep within our heart. We return like the prodigal son, *justified by God's grace as a gift, through the redemption that is in Christ Jesus, whom God put forward as a sacrifice of atonement, effective through faith.* We seek to be a servant in Our Father's house to fulfil our one desire, to serve Him, *to be steadfast, immovable, always excelling in the work of the Lord, because we know that in the Lord our labour is not in vain.* Such desire seeks a firm foundation within our intention and a promise forms in our heart, for we know that it is no longer sufficient for us to express our love in an uncertain way. We long to embrace the cleansing of spiritual poverty, the poverty that goes hand in hand with the spiritual childhood that is required for entrance into the kingdom of God. We seek the healing of emotional purity, and as we have suffered so sorely for our excuses, we long for the breadth of freedom that only true obedience brings. *Now that we have been freed from sin and enslaved to God, the advantage we receive is sanctification, the end eternal life*, and we know that the way in which we may prove our love is to be the servant of our promise.

Rom 3:24-25   1 Cor 15:58   Rom 6:22

I love to wait upon You My Lord
A servant of Your gentle counsels,
Untrained in love and skill of service
Unlearned in the letters of the law.

But yet I know the pain of years of poverty
For deep in my heart I have yearned for You,
I have burned at the fire of emotion's desire
And long for the healing that purity brings.

There is only One Master Whom I long to serve
In the breadth of the freedom of obedience,
To You alone do I turn, but a child in devotion,
For You open Your Heart to the sighing of my love.

I am that young son who abandoned his soul
And squandered Your gifts on a wayward life,
But now as I return seeking Your forgiveness
Let me but remain the servant of my promise.

Silence of Gethsemane

A loving servant watches attentively, but after a life of spiritual complacency, the servant finds this new way of service very demanding. Spiritual poverty, emotional purity and true obedience are truly hard promises to embrace, and there are moments when the challenge seems too great. In our frailty we all experience moments of doubt and hesitation but *now that we have come to know God, or rather to be known by God, how can we turn back again to the weak and beggarly elemental spirits? How can we want to be enslaved to them again?* At such times, we must cling to our faith that has been so strengthened and *take every thought captive to obey Christ*, Who never failed to go forward, setting His face towards Jerusalem despite the insistence of His followers that He was following a road that would lead to disaster. When doubts and uncertainty threaten to weaken our resolve we should *consider Him who endured such hostility against Himself so that we may not grow weary or lose heart*, and entering deep within our solitude, follow the Master into the silence of Gethsemane.

Gal 4:9   2 Cor 10:5   Heb 12:3

I love to enter the silence of Gethsemane
As doubts and uncertainty seize my troubled soul
Releasing their distress upon my poor resolve
That I might yet return to the shores of Galilee.

Their reasoning informs me that I did not know
That Your love would cause such bitter sacrifice,
But if You release me to whom shall I go
For You have the message of eternal life?

Alone and dejected with doubts as my companions
I feel their hesitation weakening my resolve,
Yet if I should linger and hearken to their plea
Who would lead me to Your eternal city?

But then I behold You standing close beside me
Holding the Chalice of Your Father's Love,
The wine that became the Blood of Redemption
Offered for my soul in the silence of Gethsemane.

Water of Life

The experience of overcoming our doubts and the prejudices we encounter, gives much encouragement to our soul as we struggle to live out our Christian vocation. *We know that suffering produces endurance, and endurance produces character, and character produces hope, and that our hope does not disappoint us, because God's love has been poured into our heart through the Holy Spirit that has been given to us.* Gradually, the anguish of the early days of our spiritual awakening, the first euphoria and the great highs and lows that followed, seem to even out, and we begin to approach the difficulties of our spiritual life in a more contemplative manner. The reason for this change is that we have, little by little, come to dwell in the love of God, with our heart drawn to Him, away from ourselves; *for since we are justified by faith, we have peace with God through Our Lord Jesus Christ, through whom we have obtained access to this grace in which we stand.* As our concern is all to love Him, we are no longer wrestling with our own nature in which He dwells, but *having received the first fruits of the Spirit, we groan inwardly while we wait for adoption, the redemption of our bodies.* We are filled with a longing that is itself an expression of our love, as we thirst for the living water that wells up to eternal life.

Rom 5:3-5   Rom 5:1-2   Rom 8:23

I love to rest at the pool by the wayside
Waiting for Your angel to breathe on the water
That I may immerse my soul in its depths
And ease the distress of the fever of my love.

I have no comfort to offer my soul
Only wordless sighs to draw Your favour,
I can only wait in longing expectation
For the water of life that will heal my soul.

It seems that the more I come to love You
The poorer is my love in my love's esteem,
And the less reassurance that I conceive
The more I thirst for the living water.

You bid me worship in Spirit and in Truth
As You lead my heart to the fount of life,
That within my soul I may draw from the spring
Of the water that wells up to eternal life.

Steps of The Sanctuary

Our longing and our thirst cause us to draw ever nearer to Our Lord as we live out our life in desire for His love. He is the treasure and the joy of our heart, and we rejoice to worship Him in the fellowship of the Holy Spirit with all the company of the saints and the angels. We come to cherish the liturgy and the life of the Church as we join with her in unending prayer and praise to the Glory of God, *who in Christ always leads her in triumphal procession and through her spreads in every place the fragrance that comes from knowing Him.* We value every opportunity to come with her before Our Saviour in the Blessed Sacrament, *for we have this hope, a sure and steadfast anchor of the soul, a hope that enters the inner shrine behind the curtain where Jesus has entered.* In this hope together we receive Him in the mystery of the Eucharist, *approaching the throne of grace with boldness, so that we may receive mercy and find grace to help in time of need;* and having received Our Lord, we remain there before Him, watching in the stillness at the steps of the sanctuary.

2 Cor 2:14   Heb 6:19-20   Heb 4:16

I love to linger as the footsteps die away
And feel the darkening shadows close around me,
Embraced by the silence and deepening solitude,
Kneeling in the stillness at the steps of the sanctuary.

I gaze through the twilight at the Sacrament reserved
Cherishing the Eucharist that gives life to my soul,
And I wonder at the mystery of Your Abiding Presence,
Enraptured by Your love that fills the longing of my heart.

You feed your disciples with the bread of the angels
As You renew Your sacrifice for the life of the world,
Dismissing all the faithful in the Power of Your Name
Whilst You lovingly remain enshrined on the altar.

I praise and worship You in the Sacrament of Heaven
Joining with the spirits in their silent adoration,
Kneeling to adore You in the presence of the angels
Watching in the stillness at the steps of the sanctuary.

Sacrament of The Moment

Christ Our Saviour is present to us in the Blessed Sacrament in a very special way, but He is always present with us on our journey of faith. We have lightened our burden so that we may travel with nothing that might hamper our spiritual discernment. We have left behind our purse of preoccupations with which we bartered with time, and have put off all the complexities of our nature that we wore to disguise our inadequacies. We *have stripped off the old self with its practices and have clothed ourselves with the new self, which is being renewed in knowledge according to the image of its creator.* We no longer wrestle with our own darkness, nor do we behave so that we might please the imagination of others for *our liberty is no longer subject to the judgement of someone else's conscience.* We are pilgrims on a journey through a fleeting world where time has no further hold over us. We look to the unending days of eternal life, and we do so with confidence *knowing that all things work together for good for those who love God, who are called according to His purpose.* For us, each day and each hour become a sacrament, the sacrament of the moment.

Col 3:9-10   1 Cor 10:29   Rom 8:28
J P Caussade: *Abandonment to Divine Providence...* "Sacrament of the moment."

I love each day, each hour, each moment,
Held in the sacrament of Your Presence,
Suspended in the silence of surrender
Above the insecurity of transient years.

Arresting the pulse of each passing moment,
Hidden envoy of Your intending providence,
You release my spirit from the burden of time
No longer held hostage by her chain of events.

You stand upon the axis of this circling world
Steadying the vertiginous centre of my soul,
For high in the immensity of Your infinite realm
I am caught up above the extent of time.

In spirit I rise towards the beams of Your radiance
That stream through the mists of eternal dawn,
I dwell in an instant of Heaven's eternity
Held in sheer wonder within the sacrament of the moment.

Summit of Holiness

Through the sacrament of the moment comes a deep and sure awareness of the loving presence of Our Saviour in all the circumstances of our life. It is as we dedicate ourselves to Our Lord in the ordinary events of every day that we become the person Our Lord intended us to be, for no longer *do we live to ourselves: if we live, we live to the Lord, and if we die, we die to the Lord, for we are the Lord's;* and it is through the hesitating steps of each day that we make the journey that leads us ever onward to our destiny, *for our citizenship is in Heaven*. Whenever we have to face the darkness of the valleys of despair, we must *recall those earlier days after we had been enlightened, and not abandon that confidence of ours, for we need endurance so that when we have done the will of God, we may receive what was promised*. While we are still clothed in mortality *we will continue to groan under our burden, not that we wish to be relieved of the garments of humanity but to be robed in vestments of salvation, so that what is mortal may be enveloped by life*. While we long for Our Lord who *will transform the body of our humiliation that it may be conformed to the body of His Glory,* we journey on in our quest for holiness, up the high mountain that rises to the Heaven of our desire. In this quest, it seems that there is always a ridge beyond the one facing us, but if we *walk by faith and not by sight* we will surely attain the summit of our journey, *Mount Zion, the city of the living God, the heavenly Jerusalem*, the summit of holiness.

Rom 14:7-8   Phil 3:20   Heb 10:32   Heb 10:35-36
2 Cor 5:4   Phil 3:21   2 Cor 5:7   Heb 12:22

I love to open my heart to the guidance of Your will
Exposing my life to the secret workings of Your Grace
And adore Your loving presence in the centre of my soul
As each day You lead me onward to the summit of my life.

Your love upholds my being on this journey of my destiny
Along the winding path through the valleys of despair,
Despite all the wanderings of my wayward spirit
You correct my direction by the compass of Your will.

You refresh me in the stream that flows beside the path
That rises to the peak of the Heaven of Your love,
You guide me in the Spirit as I make the bold ascent
And keep my steps secure upon the narrow mountain ledge.

You enlighten my mind to faith beyond poor reason's sight
With grace to persevere and to journey on in trust
Upon this path that leads beyond the ridge that lies ahead,
To there reveal my lifelong quest, the summit of holiness.

Lord Jesus,

may the sound of Your voice
greet the silence of our solitude,
and may the light of Your Presence
dispel the darkness of our vision,
that we may listen for the call of grace
and walk in the knowledge of Your Love
on this journey of our destiny
in the companionship of
the Holy Spirit.

Amen.

Of A Prisoner of Eternity

Introduction

Opening Prayer

1. Prisoner of Eternity

2. Wondrous Divinity

3. Freedom of the Kingdom of Love

4. Companion in Time

5. The Man I Feared to Be

6. A Man Awakes

7. Kinship with Immortality

8. Heart's Desire

9. Image of The Man of Heaven

10. Eternal Regeneration

Closing Prayer

Introduction

Our true identity is known only to God. We are wary of discovering ourselves too much to others, and are often embarrassed by our own self-discovery. Sometimes we are unsure as to who we are, and are even more uncertain as to the person we ought to be. Nor do we have the clarity of vision to see what we will become in the future: *now we have only glimpses of knowledge*, writes St Paul; *when the time of fulfilment comes, we shall know as fully as we are known.*

To know ourself is to discover freedom. But this freedom is not the freedom of the sons of this world: they *feel no obligation to uprightness for they are servants of sin.* Our freedom is that *we have been set free from sin and are bound to the service of God, surrendering ourselves to uprightness which is to result in sanctification.* As we willingly choose to become a servant of God we have to wrestle with our own nature within this freedom in order to discover our true identity in Christ, for it is *in Him that we find our own fulfilment.* The transformation which we undergo will lead one day to that transfiguration by which we will see ourselves as we truly are, *for our real life is Christ and when He is revealed, we will be revealed with Him in glory.*

These ten reflections and meditations are links in the chain that binds the servant of God as he attempts to interpret for himself the mystery of eternal regeneration.

The prisoner's sentence begins and ends with a prayer.

1 Cor 13:12 Rom 6:19-22 Col 2:10 Col 3:4

Lord Jesus

May the freedom of Your truth
release us from captivity,
and the reality of Your love
lead us to fulfilment,
that we may find our true identity
in the light of Your discovery,
through the secret Wisdom
of the Holy Spirit.

Amen

Prisoner of Eternity

We are, perhaps, prisoners of our own life, some would say of our own nature, some of our own desires: fundamentally we are prisoners of our own images and concepts both concerning ourselves and our spiritual life. *Christ set us free so that we should remain free, and we must not let ourselves be fastened again to the yoke of slavery.* It is in freedom that we offer ourselves to Him as willing captives, forfeiting our freedom as sons of the world *so that we may serve in the new way of the Spirit.* As we struggle with our undiscerning, unspiritual nature we look towards our eternal destiny as sons of God, *justified by the free gift of His grace through being set free in Christ Jesus.* In this spiritual freedom we reach out to the light of faith beyond the darkness of reason, prepared to remain imprisoned in the chains of our endeavour as long as mortality waits as prisoner of eternity.

Gal 5:1 Rom 7:6 Rom 3:24

I love to gaze into the immortal skies,
A prisoner awaiting his eternal destiny,
Raising my eyes from this darkened room
Where my soul lies bound in restless longing.

I hunger in my cell for the bread of life
And thirst for the cup of eternal salvation,
Longing to be filled with the sight of Your glory
Dispelling the shadows that guard mortality.

Life's earnest endeavour binds me in shackles,
My will fettered closely within these chains,
Compelling desire against darkness of reason
As I hope in Your promise of eternal freedom.

Visit me in prison with Your Risen Presence
With faith that will draw my soul to heaven,
And ease the watching of a captive's longing
Whilst mortality waits as prisoner of eternity.

Wondrous Divinity

The chains of imprisonment were to St Paul a source of freedom and inspiration, and it is good that we too should live *in captivity to the Spirit*. But it is often the case that the chains that bind us are not the restrictions that might be implied by our divine service but the inner conflicts of our stubborn will. There are many who hold fast to their chains, martyrs to their own captivity, afraid to embrace the reality of their faith in true freedom, afraid to commit themselves to *the law of the Spirit which gives life in Christ Jesus that has set us free*. It is only as we experience this sense of captivity to the Spirit that we discover that our prison is the secret chamber of Our Lord's presence where the chains that bind us are bonds of love, restraining us in our inner restlessness and securing us against our instability of faith, holding us within the mystery of His wondrous Divinity.

Acts 20:22 Rom 8:2

I love to gaze upon the Divinity of Your Being
As I languish in the chains of heavenly desire,
Listening for Your voice at the chime of each Hour
Amidst the clamour and cry of this passing world.

I hearken within to the rhythm of prayer
As I sigh for You in the depth of my soul,
My heart entranced by the heavenly chant,
The harmony of life within the reality of God.

In the secret chamber of Your hidden presence
You unfasten the chains that bind my heart,
Releasing desire by the hand of an angel
As You lead me forth by faith in Your Love.

I rise into the realms of the eternal Spirit
Where the rays of hope have drawn my soul,
And there in the heaven of my one desire
I rest in the mystery of Your wondrous Divinity.

Freedom of the Kingdom of Love

The darkened room of restless longing cannot hold us as our spirit rises above the nature of our imprisonment and ventures forth in faith into a world unknown, trusting in the infinite love of God, *for where the Spirit of the Lord is, there is freedom*. We are caught up in a sense of wonder as our awareness of the Divinity of God transcends all our earthly experience and, whilst retaining the consciousness of our humanity, we feel as if our true identity is about to be made known to us, as if *a veil were falling from our face, revealing the glory of the Lord as it reflects upon us, transforming us into His likeness with ever-increasing glory; this is the working of the Lord Who is the Spirit*, encircling us within the focus of Heaven that we may reach out to experience the true freedom of the Kingdom of Love.

2 Cor 3:17 2 Cor 3:18

I love to abandon myself to Eternity
Enfolded in prayer within the Arms of God,
Entrusting my soul to Your secret wisdom,
Resting secure in Your faithful love.

As the unseen life that lies beyond
Draws my soul by its mysterious power
I venture forth from the dwelling of humanity
Into the reality of the mystery of faith.

As You lift the veil of mortal sight
You reveal the light of eternal glory,
Resolvent rays reflecting Your likeness
Transforming the image of my immortal soul.

I stand encircled within the focus of Heaven
In the light of knowledge of eternal salvation,
A child of this world held in desire no more,
Born into the freedom of the Kingdom of Love.

Companion in Time

It is the presence of the Holy Spirit in our lives that gives us spiritual freedom, releasing our will to act according to the will of God. We are conscious of the power of grace working within us and yet, whilst *we dearly love God's law in our inmost self, we are prisoners of the law of sin which lives within us: with our mind we obey the law of God, but in our disordered nature we remain slaves to the law of sin.* We know where our true identity lies and yet we cannot hold or embrace it, for it fades as the life forces within us draw us back, focusing our attention on our human situation. We know that we need to spiritualise our life, *to live and move in the Spirit, and be guided by the Spirit*, in order that we may grasp the reality of our faith, for until we do so, we shall walk in the shadow of our real self as but a companion in time.

Rom 7:22,25 Gal 5:25

I love to wonder in the silence of surrender
At the grace You bestow upon one so frail,
And ponder in my heart the mystery of redemption
Kneeling in the confidence of Your gift of faith.

As companion of the heart of one who loves You
I walk in the assurance of his living faith,
Uncertain of the reality of the love of my heart
To freely co-operate with the inspiration of Grace.

You have chosen my companion for a mission in life,
Hesitation of mine cannot claim his attention,
Your purpose is unknown but to his heart alone
His fulfilment a vocation that invokes Your Name.

I wonder at the mystery of Your eternal Word
Written so secretly on his statement of life,
My questions and doubts cannot chain his assurance
For I walk in his shadow as but a companion in time.

The Man I Feared To Be

It is one of the greatest challenges we face, to take to ourselves the full meaning of the faith we profess, not permitting ourselves to drift through life without ever making the commitment to Our Lord which we know in our heart and mind we desire above all things. *We must put on our new self which will progress towards true knowledge the more it is renewed in the image of our Creator. We must rekindle the gift that He has given us, for God did not give us a spirit of timidity, but the Spirit of power and love and self-control,* avoiding the temptation of being like children, hiding from the challenges of faith and life behind a convenient naivety. *We are to be infants only so far as evil is concerned, but grown-ups in our thinking; as adults, we must put childish ways behind us* and grasp the reality of our true identity by accepting responsibility for ourselves, and become the man we feared to be.

Col 3:10 2 Tim 1:6-7 1 Cor 14:20 1 Cor 13:11

I love to dream with the innocence of a child
Hastening with joyful cries of greeting
As it sees You resting by the light of a lantern
On the shore of the lake in the stillness of the night.

Secretly I watch as You embrace the infant
Placing it there in the circle of light
As You look into the night from whence it came
To discover the man whom the child conceals.

I start in alarm lest the light might show me
Hiding in the darkness as a man unknown,
But as You beckon and call me by my name
A figure emerges from the shadows that surround me.

Dimly mirrored by the light of the lantern
I behold a likeness in the face of the man
For he bears the image of Your reflection,
It is the face of the man I feared to be.

A Man Awakes

The process by which we mature as Christians and adults in the world depends upon many factors, the underlying psychological effects of childhood not least amongst them. Our childish ways may now perhaps embarrass us, but those hesitating steps were all important towards our development, and we must yet continue to walk with humility. Spiritual maturity is born out of a chrysalis of ardent faith, a faith that through faith's own experience sustains us in continual growth and renewal, *for anyone who is in Christ becomes a new creation; the old order is gone, a new being is there to see.* It is a faith that has itself been nurtured and allowed to grow through the innocent trust of a child as it *comes to a knowledge of the Son of God, to its full maturity.* It is through the dreams of a child that a man awakes.

2 Cor 5:17 Eph 4:13

I love to centre my soul in Your love
And regain the balance of my steps,
Placing aside the false assurance
That weighs upon my broken resolve.

I placed conceit in imagined virtue,
Life stillborn through premature labour,
Chastened by pride and false indignation
I grieve at the death of hope ill-conceived.

I cradle my loss in a shroud of darkness
A veil drawn over the light of my faith,
In the night I bury the child of my fancies
And shiver in the shadow of myself a man.

Dawn brings its light to a new creation
Born out of a chrysalis of ardent faith,
Raised upon the hopes of heavenly desire
Through the dreams of a child a man awakes.

Kinship with Immortality

As our outer nature wastes away, inwardly we are being renewed day by day as we discover in Christ our true identity. *It is as if we have died, and now the life we have is hidden with Christ in God.* It is the transformation of a faith that fed on reassurance to a faith for which we take full responsibility, in the knowledge that to identify with Our Lord is to identify with a sign of contradiction, both within our own nature* and within the world in which we live. We stand before the Cross as a witness to Christ's resurrection, *carrying His death in our body so that His life may be visible in us; we believe and therefore we speak out, realising that He Who raised up the Lord Jesus will raise us up with Jesus in our turn, and bring us to Himself.* It is through the Cross that the Spirit of Wisdom gives life in true kinship with immortality.

2 Cor 4:16   Col 3:3   2 Cor 4:10,13-14   * Rom 7:15   Gal 5:17

I love to hide myself in Your Sacred Heart
In the secret recess of Your wounded side
Where the pain and anger of torn emotion
Are stilled in the depth of healing love.

For before I was humbled I went astray
Following a part I had cast and directed,
Seeking to establish bonds of kinship
Within gentile courts of human wisdom.

As a solitary witness I put faith on trial
Bound as a hostage to contradiction
Until I appealed to the ransom of hostility*
And turned to embrace the Cross of abjection.

For on Calvary stands the companion of witness,
Hidden from the wise in the mystery of the ages,
Harbinger through which the Spirit of Wisdom
Gives life in true kinship with immortality.

* Eph 2:16

Heart's Desire

It is through the great sign of contradiction that we learn to overcome the subtle arguments of compromise put forward by human wisdom, and come to that inner freedom of identity in which we seek the Lord in all the circumstances of our life, aware of the reality of His living presence in loving kinship. *We only want to know Christ and the power of His resurrection, and partake of His sufferings by being moulded to the pattern of His death, striving towards the goal of resurrection from the dead.* Always aware of this destiny, we live our lives to the honour of His Name knowing that here *the temporary, light burden of our hardships is earning us for ever an utterly incomparable, eternal weight of glory, since what we aim for is not visible, but invisible and eternal.* The hope that is our joy is our heart's desire.

Phil 3:10-11 2 Cor 4:17-18

I love to live out my heart's desire
To love and serve You in every way,
Open to Your will and Your commands
My desire to love You is all that I need.

My secret dream fills my heart with joy
For hidden in the future to be there revealed
I shall be like You my Risen Lord
When I shall see You as You really are.

Let me then co-operate that Grace may lead
Else I am powerless to realise my dream,
And shall die helpless with hope forlorn
Unless You first shall discover me.

To honour Your Name is my lifelong vocation
The secret aim that fills all my days,
My greatest joy is the hope unseen
That comes from the depth of my heart's desire.

Image of The Man of Heaven

Our faith is the reality of our life, for *only faith can guarantee the blessings that we hope for, or prove the existence of the realities that are unseen.* Our hope conquers all our fears as we live in the confidence of our faith, *for it is God Who has made His light shine into our hearts to enlighten them with the knowledge of God's glory, the glory on the face of Christ.* It is in the light of this knowledge that we discover our true identity and come to an awareness that *our homeland is in Heaven from where we are expecting a Saviour, the Lord Jesus Christ, who will transfigure our mortal body into the mould of His glorious body.* With this assurance, there comes the conviction that we must so live as to become more like Him each day *that just as we have borne the image of the earthly man, so we may bear the Image of the Man of Heaven.*

Heb 11:1 2 Cor 4:6 Phil 3:20-21 1 Cor 15:49

I love to lay down the tools of my labour
As each day gives way to eventide,
And rest at the wayside upon life's journey
Raising my eyes to my homeland in Heaven.

I climb the watch-tower each hour of sunset
To watch as the shadows lengthening descend,
Drawn by the wonder of the eternal day
As darkness conceals the empires of man.

At one with the company of blessed spirits
I hearken to their chorus of adoration,
In solitude attending the sound of Your voice
As I await with creation Your moment of bidding.

For You shape this desire within my heart,
Moulding my immortal soul in Your likeness,
That transformed in the light of eternal glory
I may bear the Image of the Man of Heaven.

Eternal Regeneration

Our earthly sentence, the sentence of all creation bound to decay, is remitted through the ransom paid by Our Lord. We are no longer prisoners of the world for *we have been crucified with Christ, and yet, whilst we are alive, it is no longer we who live, but Christ living in us.* We are now prisoners of eternity, *living in faith, faith in the Son of God Who loved us and gave Himself for us; groaning inside ourselves, waiting with eagerness for our whole being to be set free.* This is a mystery that is always new, hidden within the meaning of each day, a compounding of grace, its significance concealed within the eternal wisdom of God. The dawn of our salvation and the salvation of all mankind in which we bear a part, rises in our vocation to grace, and by that grace our faith grows as silently and as surely as a stalagmite in the depth our soul, building an election to eternal regeneration.

Gal 2:19-20 Rom 8:23

I love to dwell in the eternity of days
Passing beyond these moments of life,
And hearken to the continual song of the ages
Echoing high above the harmony of the universe.

I watch the unseen growth of eternal spring
Across unreclaimed continents of man's soul,
And see the shadow of the Spirit's grace
Protecting and guarding His seed of immortality.

The meaning of today is a compounding of grace,
Minute particles of sand in the hour-glass of Heaven
Concealing the significance of each passing moment
Within the hidden wisdom of our Eternal God.

Our salvation and the form of eternal days
Rises each dawn in our vocation to grace,
Stalagmite of faith in the depth of our soul
Building an election to eternal regeneration.

Lord Jesus

May the truth of our freedom
release us from captivity,
and the reality of our love
lead us to fulfilment,
that in the light of our discovery
we may find in You our true identity

through the secret Wisdom
of the Holy Spirit.

Amen

On The Unknown Reality

Introduction

Opening Prayer

1. Living Faith

2. Compulsion of Love

3. Lost Horizons

4. Need of God

5. Down by The Shore

6. Your Pain

7. A Particle of Love

8. Servant of Your Necessity

9. You Know It Lord

10. Unknown Reality

Closing Prayer

Introduction

There are moments in our spiritual life when we are faced by the awareness of the inadequacy of our faith as we struggle in our minds to secure the reality of our belief. We forget that it is not our own to hold and command: *it is by grace that we have been saved, through faith; not by anything of our own, but by a gift from God*: our faith is the often "unknown" reality in our lives.

Our faith is of ourselves only in so far as it is relative to the degree to which we respond to God, as a mirror might be angled to reflect the sun; and even then, the light of assurance that it gives is not dependant upon our perceived response to God.

Only faith can guarantee the blessings that we hope for, but the extent of our *hope* is relative to the depth of our desire for God. We have *a hope which will not let us down, because the love of God has been poured into our hearts by the Holy Spirit which has been given to us*, but often we betray the shallowness of our desire as shadows of unreality cloud our vision, enfeebling our will and preventing the freedom of our response to the inspiration of the Holy Spirit. We stumble about in a darkness in which all the familiar concepts of faith are mirrored in confusion.

These ten reflections and meditations visit this realm of uncertainty, where we know only by "unknowing"* and where we discover, through the depth of our desire and the extent of our hope, the "unknown" reality in our lives.

The meditations begin and end with a prayer.

Eph 2:8   Heb 11:1   Rom 5:5
* *T Merton:Contemplative Prayer... "unknowing"*

Lord Jesus,

May Your light
shine through the darkness
of our disbelief
revealing to us
the mystery of faith,
that we may come to You
the One Whom we desire,
the fullness of our hope
which we entrust
to the Holy Spirit
the guardian of our destiny.

Amen

Living Faith

It does not startle us to read in the writings of the saints of their humble protestations at the frailty of their faith, for we know and have studied the saintliness of their lives. And yet, we fear to admit even to ourselves that our faith is frail and instead find excuses for the circumstances that depress our spirits and weaken our perception. *With so many witnesses in a great cloud around us, we too should throw off everything that weighs us down and the sin that that clings so closely, and with perseverance keep running in the race which lies ahead of us, fixing our eyes on Jesus, Who leads us in our faith and brings it to perfection.* To follow the example of the saints in the way of Our Saviour requires us to be open with God and honest with ourselves if we are to discover the reality of a living faith.

Heb 12:1-2

I love to feel the assurance of Your love
As I am startled by the shadow of my disbelief,
Discovering anew the frailty of my faith
In the face of the pain of life's experience.

As the shallowness of my reasoning fails
In response to a greater depth of discovery,
I struggle with the concepts of my belief
And confess my shame and inadequacy.

Yet in the darkness of my questioning
I touch upon the mystery of faith,
That You were born into the universe for man
To perfect our faith through Your suffering. *

Such knowledge of You challenges my reason
And tests the depth of my understanding
As I awaken to the truth that releases shame
And discover the reality of a living faith.

* Luke 18:31 Jesus talks to His disciples
concerning His suffering and death

Compulsion of Love

The reality of a living faith is tested in the events of each day. It is when we most need to pray, to acknowledge the Presence of Our Lord, whether at rest or in activity, that we often find ourselves so torn by emotion, depressed or distracted by our cares and activities that we hesitate and let the moment pass. We then sink into even deeper distress, and as nostalgia for prayer burdens our spirit we turn away from God - just for a moment - as our inclination turns to resistance. We are impatient of His call upon us, we resent being constrained, and in our moment of pride we forget that we have *no righteousness of our own but only that which comes through faith in Christ, the righteousness from God based on faith.* As we experience the pain of the inadequacy of our love, *let us draw near to God with a sincere heart in full assurance of faith*, for such is the pain that needs above all things to accept the compulsion of love.

Phil 3:9   Heb 10:22

I love to kneel in the companionship of silence
When I have stayed the pride of my activity
And calmed my mind of its restless will
To listen within to the invitation of love.

It is the spiralling tasks of a worldly order,
With demands that argue for immunity from prayer,
That once entertained offer my refusal
To the banquet prepared in honour of Your Name.

As nostalgia wells up in the hesitance of regret
The tensions increase to justify their claim,
And the capacity for the Spirit to guide my heart
Diminishes to needlepoint, a thread of desire.

Then in the darkness of the ensuing pride
My spirit searches the streets of the town,
Wandering the deserted lanes and byways
Waiting for the servant of the compulsion of love.*

* Luke 14:15 The parable of the great banquet

Lost Horizons

The compulsion of love first demands a willing spirit but we know how great a level of resistance we can offer - except in the case of distress and disaster: they have their own way of bringing a man to his knees, even when the call to faith has remained unanswered for a lifetime. It is when events are beyond our power or beyond the control of our will that we are unable to prevent our cry to the One Whom we then acknowledge to be greater than ourselves. This awakening to the experience of faith does not only occur in times of human crisis but, particularly, in faith's own crisis. Whether throughout our lives or in just one moment of resistance, *we all have been estranged and hostile to God, but Jesus has reconciled us by His death to bring us before Himself faultless and irreproachable - as long as we persevere and stand firm on the solid base of faith, never letting ourselves drift away from the hope promised by the Gospel.* However, there are times when we are unable to find our bearings, adrift and helpless upon the ocean of life amidst lost horizons.

Col 1:21-23

I love to know that You are in the stern of the boat *
As I am tossed on a sea of conflicting desires,
The external forces of wind and sea raging
Amidst the heaving and turbulence of my inner being.

Life sickness and fearful agitation surround me
Yet I know that You alone whilst quietly sleeping
Are watching for the hour when the storms overtake me
And in the extreme of dismay I turn to You.

Is not this life but a voyage through darkest faith
Across the deepest oceans of hidden reason?
Then what matters discomfort of earthly heart
If my soul may rest in the sureness of faith!

So I gaze into the darkness from the stern of the boat
My pounding heart aching with eternal longing
As I journey through the torrents and heavy seas
Upon the ocean of life amidst lost horizons.

Mark 4:37 Jesus calms the storm

Need of God

Lost horizons make us aware of the reality of our need of God, and we have learnt that it is *in Christ Jesus Our Lord and through faith in Him that we may approach God with freedom and confidence.* It is Jesus alone Who can give life its meaning, its sense of direction, Who alone can satisfy the hidden longing of our hearts. Human longings can never satisfy the insatiable thirst of our created spirit, which is drawn to the One Eternal Source of Love as witnessed for us in creation, as discovered to us in the holy scriptures, as ever present with us in the most Blessed Sacrament. *As we have received Christ Jesus the Lord, so we must continue to live our lives in Him, rooted and built up in Him and established in faith.* Let us no longer hesitate to acknowledge our frailty but bow down before Our Saviour admitting the confusion in our hearts, and confess our need of God.

Eph 3:12   Col 2:6-7

I love to weep in the silence of solitude
As I nurse the wound of the pain of love,
Crushed by the burden of my humanity
My soul cries out for its Saviour God.

Amidst the shadows of a darkened world
I carry my awareness of my need of God,
The essence of all my hopes and desires
As I strain to touch the reality of faith.

I turn from my darkness with tearful cry
Into the brightness of the Eternal Presence, *
As on the altar of love Your pain releases
The healing of faith on my human despair.

I reach out to touch the most Blessed Sacrament
Wherein lies concealed the recognition of faith,
My soul weeping for joy in its eternal desire,
My heart embracing my need of God.

** Luke 1: 78-79 the Rising Sun will come to shine on those
             living in darkness and the shadow of death*

Down by The Shore

It is through the turmoil of a heart's need for God that we truly mature as Christians and become followers of Our Lord. As we take responsibility for our faith we discover that our life is in our hands that we may offer it to Our Lord. Only in seeking Christ our true fulfilment will we achieve our full potential, will *our faith continue to grow and the area of its influence expand*, for such is the desire that needs to express itself in service. Perhaps we have not yet found that vocation or repose of soul in which we may uncover the depth of our faith: perhaps we have been trying to find our own way instead of listening for guidance in the silence of our own hearts. *Faith comes from hearing the message, and the message is heard through the word of Christ.* We must put to one side our own statements concerning our spiritual life and, sure of His awareness of our loving attention, listen to Jesus as He teaches His disciples down by the shore.

2 Cor 10:15   Rom 10:17

I love to listen by the path near the lakeside
As You teach Your disciples the mysteries of Heaven,
Your voice drifting softly over the rippling waters
From the boat that is anchored not far from the shore. *

I hear all Your words as if spoken to me
As silently I enter a world far remote
From the needs of imagined desire and emotion
That cause such division in my search for peace.

As a lonely traveller on the quest of faith
I have nowhere to call my spirit's home,
For this world cannot furnish the sanctuary of my dreams,
There is no earthly place where my longings find rest.

I rise to my feet as the boat drifts from the land
And watch as Your disciples set sail to windward,
Your solitary figure acknowledging my greeting
As I follow along the path down by the shore.

*Math 13:2 Such large crowds gathered that Jesus got into a boat
while all the people stood listening on the shore*

Your Pain

Our lonely path of faith leads us into many unknown and uncertain ways in which we pray for grace and guidance. It is a quest that cannot be measured by a worldly sense of wellbeing or of achievement, for *it depends on faith, in order that the promise may rest on grace.* The traveller alone knows his inner conviction that brings contentment, his own purpose which conveys its own measure of achievement. Nor can his way be judged by any particular degree of conformity: *a man is not justified by such observations, but by faith in Jesus Christ.* Anything that he may achieve and any inner consolation that he may be granted, become an offering to God. The fulfilment of faith is our destiny, the way of faith to accept that joy in everything in Our Lord's service which brings the grace and privilege of sharing His pain.

Rom 4:16   Gal 2:16

I love to place all my hope in You
As I kneel in the darkness of despair,
In my prayer for the tenderness of Your mercy
I seek grace and guidance to journey on.

Your act of mercy is to cast Your robe
Around my cold and trembling shoulders
As I seek to bear the pain of Your suffering
On the path of life You bade me walk.

I do not seek release from my journey,
No chosen grace or special privilege,
But purely the knowledge that Your Love
Will sustain me in this life long service.

For the eternal destiny of my being
Lies in abandonment to Your Providence,
The way of faith that joy in everything *
Which brings the grace and privilege of sharing Your pain.

* Fr Christian de Chergé (Atlas Martyr)
   "for the sake of that joy in everything and in spite of everything"

A Particle of Love

The apostles and the martyrs, amidst much personal pain and anguish, bore the message of faith in their lives for all to see, and today the apostolic spirit continues to bear witness in the life of the Church. A few are called to heroic service and sacrifice, but many more are chosen to become hidden martyrs of love in their daily lives. We all can offer our ordinary lives to Our Saviour in total selflessness wherever we may be, *the faith that we have being our own conviction before God*, bearing witness that *we have been crucified with Christ and no longer live, but Christ lives in us; that the life we are living in the body we live by faith in the Son of God, Who loved us and gave Himself for us*, and thus become, in evidence to the faith we profess, a particle of love.

Rom 14:22   Gal 2:19-20

I love to hope that the little that I am
May fall as a grain upon the ocean sands,
Unseen by man as he walks the shore
Hidden evidence of love beneath his feet.

To suffer swirling tides and battering gales,
Amid tossing seas and crashing waves,
Between vast boulders and jagged rocks
To fall and there be finely crushed.

On winter flood-tides to drift unseen
Amidst watery plant and debris torn,
In summer heat to lie baked and dry
There lost with every semblance gone. *

And then within the Hand that strains
Each grain of finely sifted sand,
Freely through the fingers of eternity
To fall in evidence as a particle of love.

* *Mat 16:25 Whoever wants to save his life will lose it,*
    but whoever loses his life for Me will find it

Servant of Your Necessity

That our lives may be given in evidence to the love of God is the call to the fulfilment of our faith. *The only thing that counts is faith expressing itself through love*, and thus we no longer live our lives for ourselves: *our work is produced by faith, our labour prompted by love, our endurance inspired by our hope in our Lord Jesus Christ*. Whatever gifts we have been given *prepare us for works of service so that the body of Christ may be built up until we all reach unity in the faith and in the knowledge of the Son of God and become mature, attaining to the whole measure of the fullness of Christ*. If the Spirit has been given to us for the continuance of the work of the saving Passion of Our Lord, then we are to become servants of Christ's necessity.

Gal 5:6   1 Thes 1:3   Eph 4:12-13

I love to believe that the little that I do
May be filled with the service that You desire,
That whatever I conceive may be born out of love
Without thought of merit nor by virtue striven.

I pray that my offering be the spirit of my nature,
Unfettered generosity through a faithful heart,
That You may recognise but a single motive
Shining with the reflection of Your Heavenly Love.

For what I do matters not in my service for You
As in Your Hand rests the Sceptre of Omnipotence,
My heart's sole desire in the gift of my love
Is to offer a cup of water to ease Your thirst. *

Increase the quantity of bread as I break it
Multiply it for me the more freely that I share,
That the riches of Your poverty that lie in Your bounty
May fill the hands of the servant of Your necessity.

** Math 25:35 For I was hungry and you gave Me something to eat,
   I was thirsty and you gave me something to drink*

Mark 9:41   a cup of water in My Name

You Know It Lord

For our service of the Lord to be truly in fulfilment of our vocation we must be sure of our motive and our intention, and of the firmness of our faith, *for without faith it is impossible to please God, since anyone who comes to Him must believe that He exists and that He rewards those who earnestly seek Him.* It requires more than an outward statement, but an inner conviction in deep humility. *We must never pride ourselves on being better than we really are, but think of ourselves dispassionately, recognising that God has given to each of us our measure of faith.* Our Lord tests the faith of all who would serve Him, but before all things Jesus desires to prove our love, seeking our protestation that we may know in our heart of hearts the depth of our love for Him, such that we too can cry "You know it Lord".

Heb 11:6   Rom 12:3

I love to feel Your Eyes upon me
Testing to see if I really love You,
Seeking my tears and protestation,
For You know it Lord, You know that I love You. *

The Spirit searches the desires of my heart
To see if truly this man is true,
To test that the mind, the heart and will
Are burning with such love, true love for You.

As the tears well deeply I bow my head
Absorbed in a sigh of eternal desire,
The cry to possess the unknown reality
The faith of all the faithful who truly love You.

The Spirit takes my love in all its anguish
My being suspended in this one desire
As I hear my voice thrice echo in my heart
"You know it Lord, You know that I love You".

* *John 21:17 Lord, You know all things;*
     You know that I love You.

Unknown Reality

With these words we enter into the mystery of faith through which *we have been justified and have found peace with God through our Lord Jesus Christ.* Not by our own efforts, but *through Him, we have gained access by faith into this grace in which we now stand, and we rejoice in the hope of the glory of God.* Filled with desire we turn to Our Heavenly Father *in the faith and love that spring from this hope that is stored up for us in heaven,* sure in the knowledge that *the reality is found in Christ.* Through the silence and the darkness, in the stillness of "unknowing", we have discovered the depth of our desire and the extent of our hope and are now absorbed within the mystery of the Unknown Reality.

Rom 5:1-2   Col 1:5   Col 2:17

I love the silence of the night of faith
Where the centre of all meaning dwells,
Hidden in the darkness from my reason
Coerced into the stillness of unknowing.

In this silence of my senses
The parade of urgent passers by
Is hushed, and all that does remain
Is held suspended in my inmost being.

There is no force or pressing power
To overcome, nor questioning arise,
For my soul is abandoned freely
In life or death no shadows fearing.

Within this fast of consolation
Filled with hunger for eternal fulfilment,
I discover the depth of my desire for Your love
Absorbed within the mystery of the Unknown Reality.

Lord Jesus,

May Your light
shine through the darkness
of our unknowing
revealing to us
the reality of faith,
that we may come to You
the One Whom we desire
in Whom rests all our hope
which is held in trust for us
by the Holy Spirit,
the guardian of our salvation.

Amen

Seasonal Meditations

Introduction

Opening Prayer

1. Queen of Heaven

2. Universal Mother of Salvation

3. The Star of Immortality

4. A Child of God

5. The Tapestry of God

6. A Bystander

7. Silhouette of God

8. In The Shadow of The Cross

9. In the Palm of My Hand

10. On the Road to Emmaus

11. The Seamless Robe of Grace

12. The Essence of Your Soul

13. Atlas of The World

Closing Prayer

Introduction

Throughout the years of our life, the festivals of the Church's calendar are signposts on our journey towards God. As the events that are celebrated are brought before us in the Gospels, we have the joy of contemplating these special moments and their significance in our spiritual lives.

Our perception changes as our faith develops, and each year we find that one particular aspect of the mystery celebrated carries new meaning for us. There is no risk of familiarity, for the deeper our faith, the deeper our perception becomes. Our appreciation of the mysteries that surround us each and every day is heightened through the meaning we perceive in each renewed celebration.

These meditations are like little windows in the advent calendar of our faith, opening to reveal the rays of another dawn, opening to cast a little more light upon our understanding.

Each meditation begins and ends with a prayer.

Lord Jesus,

Grant that in our daily living
within the world around us,
we may ever see reflected
the mystery of Your Love
which we celebrate with wonder
on this special day of festival,
in the Holy Spirit's rejoicing
within our hearts of faith.

Amen

Queen of Heaven

In all our sorrow and through all our anxiety and suffering, there is one special person who smiles down upon us, loving us for all our faltering steps and childlike ways as we follow along the path she trod, the path of true devotion to her beloved Son, Our Saviour Jesus Christ. The eyes of Mary, Our Mother, watch over us as they watched over her Son in the days of His Manhood; and her smile and her affection comfort and console us, her prayers ever with us, supporting and encouraging us. As we dream of the day when she may greet us in Paradise, we raise our pilgrim eyes to behold her, assumed into glory in the company of Our Blessed Lord, and watch as she is led before the King, honoured by all creation, the Queen of Heaven.

I love to dream as a pilgrim in Paradise
Of the Mother of Our Lord assumed into Glory,
Silhouette against the sun in the highest Heaven
A sign of sure hope and of solace to mankind.

Glorified by the Most High above all creation
She is led to the King with her maiden companions,
Escorted amid gladness and shouts of joy
She carries the sceptre of her Royal Son.

Her robes are fragrant with aloes and myrrh
In tribute to the years when sadness adorned her,
Richly embroidered with pearls set in gold
Reflecting the beauty of her immaculate soul.

Life could not hold her nor death overtake
The one who was chosen, highest honour of our race,
To bear the Child Who gave life to the world,
Loving Mother of Salvation, Queen of Heaven.

Universal Mother of Salvation

There is for us one special person with whom we share our love of the Lord all the days of our life, the Virgin Mary. In our continual longing for redemption, we are drawn to Mary who holds the unique position as the one chosen by God to bear His Son, Our Saviour. Her love and the prayers of her Immaculate Heart embrace us in our desire for holiness. It is our humble joy and our devotion to unite ourselves to her at the moment of her consecration to God and to dedicate ourselves to her, the Universal Mother of Salvation.

I love the beauty of your holiness
Immaculate daughter of God's grace,
I rise into the realms of the Spirit
To greet you at Our Lord's conception.

As I kneel before you in deep devotion
I pray to you for regeneration
That united to your angel greeting
I may conceive a child of grace.

My soul reformed in this recreation
Cries out to you at its infant birth
Foster this child that it may become
An orphan for Our Lord's adopting.

To you I dedicate this child of grace
In consecration to our Saviour,
A child of your interceding love
Universal Mother of Salvation.

The Star of Immortality

High upon the summit of our soul, we hear the angel voices telling of the birth of Our Saviour, and gaze out into the night of our mortality to behold the Star of Bethlehem, shining from the eternal realms of Heaven upon the Child of God, cradled in innocence, bathed in the radiance of the Star of Immortality.

I love to behold the Star of Immortality,
The Star of our hope over Bethlehem,
Heavenly radiance that reveals to mankind
The paradigm of our eternal salvation.

I gaze on the Star resplendent with glory
Piercing the darkness of our mortality,
Manifestation of the eternal promise
Of undying days in the intimacy of God.

In deep consciousness of love I see before me
Enshrined in a lowly tabernacle of innocence
The Light of All Nations conceived as a Child,
The humble cradle of the world's redemption.

As the light from the Star penetrates my vision
Manifesting the intimacy of God's secret design,
I worship the Child of our eternal salvation
Bathed in the radiance of the Star of Immortality.

A Child of God

As we kneel before Our Saviour in His Nativity, we pray that He may be born in our soul and conform us to His likeness, completing in us the mystery of His incarnation, making it possible for us to live an interior spiritual life, hidden with Him in God; and that by His indwelling, He may bring to perfection in us the mysteries of His Passion and Cross by calling us to share in His suffering and death, that we may rise with Him to everlasting life. It is through the mystery of the Nativity of the Son of God that we come to new birth, as a child of the resurrection, a child of God.

I love to cradle You in Your Mother's arms
Incarnate Son of the Eternal Father,
And worship You the Child of our nativity
As I embrace this moment of our visitation.

Enlarge my heart that I may receive You
Born in my soul for my sanctification,
That my life may be hidden in the temple of God,
Enfolded within the womb of Eternity.

By Your holy indwelling teach me the mysteries
On the path by which You were glorified,
That I may share in the Bread from Your table
And drink from the Cup of eternal salvation.

Through the Divine Motherhood of Our Blessed Lady
Bestow on me the Image of Eternity,
That I may become through this visitation
A child of the resurrection, a child of God.

The Tapestry of God

Woven as upon a tapestry, the pattern of the fulfilment of the Scriptures, its meaning hidden throughout the ages within the design of God, is revealed to us by the light of revelation at the birth of Our Saviour. Born according to the line of David, but in a humble stable, God revealed His Son as the Messiah. He bore the honour and the glory of God, yet lay enfolded in Our Lady's arms in the swaddling clothes of humanity. As we gaze upon the line of eternal generation, woven through the mystery of the incarnation, we pray that our life may be a thread of love upon the tapestry of God.

I love to discover in the meaning of this day
The mystery of the pattern of the tapestry of God,
The design that was hidden in the wisdom of the ages,
Fulfilled in the love that is manifest today.

The Light of the world that was in the beginning
Born to us this day in a stable of Bethlehem,
Revealed in the flesh yet concealed in nature,
The Son of God incarnate in the cloak of humanity.

In the radiance of the Star whose beams from eternity
Shine upon Redemption cradled in infancy,
I behold the Messiah of the lineage of David
The Son of Man enfolded in the garment of salvation.

Tracing the intricate line of eternal generation
The design of the pattern on this fabric of faith,
I pray that my life may be a thread of love
Woven by Your Hand upon the tapestry of God.

A Bystander

How often do we gaze on the scene of the Nativity of Our Lord, or kneel before the crib in awe and amazement at our Incarnate God! The mystery overtakes us, for as we behold the Christ-child with His Mother we are overwhelmed at the wonder - and the simplicity of it all. As with the generations that watched for the coming of the Messiah, we are never ready for such a moment of revelation, but are, as it were, a bystander discovered upon a floodlit stage.

I love to kneel in the silence of the night
Hesitant pilgrim in the stable at Bethlehem,
Bystander discovered upon a floodlit stage
As the hush betrays our Saviour's Presence.

As one overtaken by such love conceived
Through the election of His Chosen Lady,
I gaze in awe at Our God concealed
In humble poverty for man's enrichment.

Overwhelmed by the intention of the Father's love,
The escrow of life for man's redemption,
I witness the deed of the promised fulfilment
The gift of life to be sealed with His blood.

The angels reveal what my eyes fail to see
Our God descended within the soul of man,
The reflection of Heavenly sanctity on earth
Shining upon the bystander who kneels by the crib.

Silhouette of God

In Jesus we see, through the shadows of Gethsemane and the darkness of Calvary, the reflected image of the Godhead from before the dawn of time, the Son of Man taking upon Himself the Cross of humanity's frailty and sinfulness, confronting the forces of evil for man's redemption. We gaze through the darkness, and against the intensity of salvation's aurorean sky, we behold the Silhouette of God.

I love to behold You amidst the shadows of the Garden,
Silhouette of God against the gathering clouds of night,
Eidolon of the Godhead from before the dawn of time
Communing with Your Father from within the Heart of Man.

I can only sense the depth of love's consuming anguish
In which Your earthbound Soul in longing for fulfilment
Seeks to free enslaved mankind and open Heaven's way
By the wounds that man inflicts upon the chosen Lamb of God.

The baptism of suffering that awaits Your Father's bidding
Draws tears of bitter grief in desolation from Your Heart
As You prepare to be the One to witness to His Holiness
In the agony which man conceives as tribute to his God.

I watch with all creation in trembling for redemption
As You offer to Your Father the sacrifice of love,
Raised above the darkened hill against the aurorean sky
I behold You there upon the Cross the Silhouette of God.

In The Shadow of The Cross

As we contemplate Our Saviour hanging upon the Cross, we are torn with grief and bewilderment. How could it be that He should have been caused to die for such sins as ours, of which we take so little account? It is as if He had to die before our eyes for us to believe that our sinfulness so deserves the wrath of the Almighty God. We are not worthy to even contemplate His sufferings and yet we are drawn to gaze upon Him dying on the Cross with a love we cannot contain. The cause of His death pierces our soul with shame, the wound releasing our longing for His love and our desire for holiness as we kneel in the shadow of the cross.

I love to kneel in the shadow of Your Cross
In the surest knowledge that Your Resurrection
Is the meaning and the end of this evil triumph
In which our sins sought to destroy the Son of God.

At the sight of Your wounded hands I cry with loathing
That such sins as mine should have merited this,
For as it was I that hungered for the tree of life
Then as surely as I love You it was I that betrayed You.

My darkened soul may not share Our Lady's bitter grief
For the sword that pierced her soul lies at my feet,
But for the mercy of this moment as I kneel before You
I should have died the traitor's death on unhallowed ground.

It is by the Cross on which You die that hope remains
For my sins that paid the price are crucified in You
You ransom me from death and from the serpent's deadly curse
And take my soul to Yourself in the shadow of Your Cross.

In the Palm of My Hand

For many Christians the Cross casts a shadow across their lives, a shadow which they fear and do not understand. The re-enactment of the Passion is itself a trial of their faith, its meaning and mystery hidden by their lack of recognition of themselves in Jesus - with Peter and the other disciples, they question the need for such a sacrifice. It is only when we learn to identify with Jesus that we are able to recognise the figure upon the Cross. As in that moment of intimacy when we receive Our Lord in the Eucharist, it is through faith we see Him and by faith we hold Him in the palm of our hand.

I love to hold the Cross in the palm of my hand,
And feel the touch of intimacy as softly I trace
The figure of my Beloved upon His blessed image,
My finger lingering long upon His sacred wounds.

The image of Our Saviour set before my eyes
The immensity of God the focus of my gaze,
In tender communion as in the Eucharistic feast
The substance of Your love held within my grasp.

In secret You reveal the excellence of Your dignity
That the shame of Your Passion may not weaken my faith,
You show me the nature of the change I must undergo
That I too may share in the honour of the Cross.

I gaze upon the instrument of the notoriety of love
High pillar standing silhouette against life's setting sun,
Whose cruel arms did hold the One I now embrace
The figure of my Beloved in the palm of my hand.

On the Road to Emmaus

We can only imagine the confusion and dismay in the hearts of the disciples when their Master was led to His death by the soldiers of the Roman Empire amid the triumphant shouts of the religious hierarchy. His followers, men of innocence and goodness who had pledged Him their love and their loyalty, could only stand by in fear and watch as they condemned Him. Let us measure their grief by the depth of their love, and ask ourselves how often we have pledged our loyalty and turned away, unsure of the reality of our love, and remain in close companionship with Our Lord, living out our life amidst the mystery of revelation on the road to Emmaus.

I love to linger in the shadows on the road to Emmaus
Where the anguish of my heart sought solace in my grief,
For standing by in fear I had watched as they condemned Him,
Witness to the wounds that pierced the Chosen One of God.

The prophets had foretold the suffering of God's Servant
In the shame and desolation of such a death as His,
I had listened to His words but did not heed their warning
That it was He who was destined to suffer for mankind.

I shared the shadows of my path with a stranger unawares
Who recalled the words of prophecy as if they were His own,
He filled my heart with burning hope as He spoke of Atonement
And of the Rising of the One to Whom I had pledged my love.

I could not restrain my tears at that moment of perception
When I recognised His Presence in the breaking of the bread,
For in this Blessed Sacrament He revealed Himself to me
In the mystery of revelation on the road to Emmaus.

The Seamless Robe of Grace

In the silence of the garden at the dawn of Our Lord's Resurrection, unobserved by the shrouded women and the attendant disciples until all had been accomplished, the angels watched over the entrance to the tomb. They had been close beside their Master in His Agony in the garden of Gethsemane and had wept at His Hour upon the Cross. Now, in the joy of His Resurrection, waiting for Him as He discarded the linen cloths within the tomb, they laid out for Him in a corner close by, His tear-stained robe, a symbol of the spirit and authority of the Son of Man, the Mantle of His earthly life, the Seamless Robe of Grace.

I love to walk with angels in the shadows of the garden
To the corner of the rock near the entrance to Your tomb,
For it was there on a stone that I saw Your Seamless Robe
As if discarded by the guard yet neatly placed aside.

It had lain undiscovered in that corner of the garden
Near the shrouded figures of the women softly weeping,
Concealed from the eyes of Your attendant disciples
As they came there to witness Your glorious Resurrection.

The dew lay soft upon its folds moistening Your tears
As they boldly crossed the threshold of the Holy Sepulchre,
Unnoticed as they entered the place whereon You rested
Witnessing the linen cloths which You had there discarded.

And in that wondrous moment I turned towards the stone
But no Robe was there and in its place no mark upon the dew,
It was the work of angels who had laid it there for You..
The Mantle of the Son of Man, the Seamless Robe of Grace.

The Essence of Your Soul

As we draw near to Our Saviour in the Blessed Sacrament we reach out to Him from the depth of our soul, worshipping and adoring the Risen Son of God, longing to receive Him in the most holy Eucharist that we may be nourished by His Body and Blood. Earnestly we unite ourselves to Jesus in His Passion, beseeching Him that He will cleanse us and strengthen us in our frailty, sustaining us in our faith and guarding us from all evil. Then reaching out to receive Our Lord, rising in desire for His Loving Embrace, our soul fills with longing that one day He may bid us come to Him that with the angels and saints we may praise forever the Essence of His Soul.

Based upon the prayer "Anima Christi"
(Literal translation, Treasury of Devotion, 1869)

I love to worship the Essence of Your Soul
Which sanctifies my lowly dwelling
As I eat of the bread of Your Risen Body,
The life You offered to redeem my soul.

I drink of Your Blood which fills the chalice
With the wine that will raise my heart to heaven,
And bathe my soul with the Water of Life
To cleanse and heal the wounds of my sin.

I gaze on Your Face in Your Passion's anguish
And pray that Your Grace may strengthen me,
That when I cry in the pain of my frailty
You may comfort my soul and stay close by my side.

Let me then touch the Wounds in Your Hands
And hide in Your Heart all my doubts and fears,
So that united through faith to Your sacrifice
Nothing may discerp my soul from Your Love.

Guard this dwelling from inhabitation by evil
And defend my heart from the tempter's cunning,
That I may abide in the stillness of Your Presence
Listening for Your call as my hour draws nigh.

Then open my ears to the Sound of Your Voice
Bidding me come to Your Loving Embrace
That I may join with the angels and saints
Praising forever the Essence of Your Soul.

ATLAS of the World

From the hidden world of Algeria the words of Fr Christian continue to echo around the globe as the witness of the Seven Brothers rises over the Atlas of the world...

Lord,

I love to remember these friends that You gave us
Martyrs to the love that is dearer than life,
Chosen by the Spirit for the salvation of souls
Witnesses hidden amidst the continents of men.

The lives that they led bore the risk of true faith
Their being surrendered to the will of God,
Lives that were GIVEN as an offering of love
Lost for the sake of that JOY in everything.

The death they accepted as they bid A-DIEU
Was the final testimony of their mission in life,
To establish communion by the Gift of the Spirit
Refashioning the likeness in the face of God.

For all their friends of yesterday and today,
Many hundredfold granted than was promised,
Their gaze is immersed in that of the Father,
Witnesses risen over the Atlas of the world.

Written to commemorate the deaths of seven Cistercian monks martyred 21st May 1996 at the monastery of Our Lady of Atlas, Algeria. Words and theme to reflect the spiritual testimony of Fr. Christian de Chergé, Prior, which was opened after his death and published on the internet.

Lord Jesus,

Grant that in our daily living
within the world around us,
we may ever see reflected
the mystery of Your Love
which we celebrate with wonder
throughout the Church's year,
in the Holy Spirit's rejoicing
within our hearts of faith.

Amen

Appendix

To record the dates

Collections

On The Love of God	October 1994
On The Longing for God	July 1995
On The Journey to God	July 1996
Of A Prisoner of Eternity	July 1997
On The Unknown Reality	July 1998

Seasonal Poems

Queen of Heaven	Assumption 1996
Universal Mother of Salvation	Immaculate Conception 1994
The Star of Immortality	Christmas 1995
A Child of God	Christmas 1995
The Tapestry of God	Christmas 1996
A Bystander	Christmas 1997
Silhouette of God	Easter 1996
In The Shadow of The Cross	Easter 1995
In the Palm of My Hand	Easter 1998
On the Road to Emmaus	Easter 1997
The Seamless Robe of Grace	Easter 1996
The Essence of Your Soul	August 1995
Atlas of The World	May 21st 1998